Painting
with tempera

Paige Henson

The Rourke Press, Inc.
Vero Beach, Florida 32964

ART CREDITS:
© Corel: pages 4, 20, 26;
© Eyewire, Inc.: pages 17, 23
Joseph Pinaud: pages 8, 12, 13, 14, 18, 22, 23, 24, 25; Freddie Mahler: page 13

PHOTOGRAPHY:
Glen Benson and East Coast Studios

PRODUCED & DESIGNED BY:
East Coast Studios, Merritt Island, Florida

EDITORIAL SERVICES:
Susan Albury

ACKNOWLEDGEMENTS:
East Coast Studios would like to thank Gardendale Elementary School, Merritt
Island, for their assistance in this project.

Library of Congress Cataloging-in-Publication Data

Henson, Paige, 1949-
    Painting with tempera / by Paige Henson
        p. cm. — (How to paint and draw)
    Includes bibliographical references and index.
    Summary: Provides techniques and advice on painting with tempera and
suggests several projects to try.
    ISBN 1-57103-311-4
    1. Tempera painting—Technique Juvenile literature. [1. Tempera painting—
technique. 2. Painting—Technique.] I. Title. II. Series: Henson, Paige, 1949-
How to paint and draw.
ND2468.H46 1999
751.4'3—dc21   99-30658
                                                           CIP

Printed in the USA

Contents

How Old Is Painting?

Thousands of years ago, even before what we call "history" began, the first pictures and drawings were painted on the walls and ceilings of dark caves. This prehistoric cave art often showed antelopes, bison, mammoths, and other wild animals that were hunted for food by early humans.

Cave paintings were made by early humans even before recorded history.

Cavemen probably did not think of these early pictures as art or decoration as we do. More likely they felt that art was a kind of magic that would help them capture and control the wild game that was essential for survival.

PROJECT

Many years ago people had to use whatever they could find to create art. Use your imagination and think of everyday things you could use to apply **tempera** (TEM puh ruh) paint. Natural materials like a twig, a fresh leaf, a feather, pine needles, or similar objects are best.

CHAPTER 2 Watch Your Tempera!

Painting with tempera is easy and fun. The colors are so deep and bright you can even paint on brown paper or cardboard, even though you'll probably want to use white paper. Here's what you'll need to begin:

1 A smock or old shirt to cover your clothes

2 Newspaper to place under the paper or under the easel (if you're using one)

3 A **palette** (PAL ut). If you don't have an artist's palette, a muffin tin, a plate, or just about anything will do.

4 Paper towels

5 Paint brushes

6 Jar of water

7 A Popsicle stick, tongue depressor, or similar object to use as a **palette knife** (PAL ut NYF)

8 Tempera paints come in a premixed liquid form, in cakes to be mixed with water, and even in marker pens with sponges at the tips.

9 Paper of your choice (newsprint or white paper in a size larger than notebook paper is best)

Which Way to Paint?

Whether you're painting on an easel or a tabletop, decide which way to turn your paper—vertically (up-and-down), or horizontally (sideways). A painting of something tall will probably need to be **vertical** (VUHR tuh kul). If your picture is more wide than tall, you will need more **horizontal** (hohr uh ZAHN tul) space.

Using Brushes

For the best results, remember to wet your brush and dry it with a paper towel before dipping it into the tempera paint. Wipe any excess paint from your brush before applying it to your paper. If you are changing colors, wash the brush by stirring it gently at the bottom of your water container, then wipe the rinsed brush with a paper towel before beginning a new color.

Cool Tips

When painting, be careful not to press so hard with your brush that you're not using the hairs of the brush at all! Keep a fresh supply of paint on your brush and you won't be tempted to "push" for the color.

Other Utensils—Use Your Imagination!

Cardboard roll
This is a great way to create a perfect circle.

Household sponge
Sponges cut into various shapes—clovers, hearts, half moons, etc.—can be dipped in tempera poured onto a paper plate, then sponged on paper to create designs.

Cotton swabs
These are great for making dots and dashes of color.

Toothbrush
Dip the bristles into paint that has been poured onto a paper plate. Very carefully flick the paint onto your paper to create a splattered effect.

CHAPTER 3

The Color Wheel

There are three basic or primary colors from which all other colors begin: red, yellow, and blue. These colors cannot be mixed from other colors but must be produced from nature's pigments such as ground animal, vegetable, or mineral sources combined with oil or a gum substance from trees.

The three secondary colors are orange, green, and purple. Each secondary color is created by mixing equal amounts of the two primary colors on either side of it on the color wheel, like this:

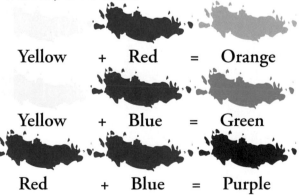

Yellow	+	Red	=	Orange
Yellow	+	Blue	=	Green
Red	+	Blue	=	Purple

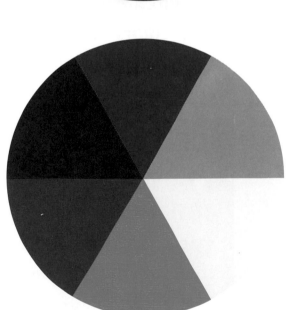

11

Plus there are many colors in between. Intermediate colors are made by mixing a primary and a secondary color together. Intermediate colors are:

yellow-orange   red-orange
red-violet (purple) blue-violet (purple)
blue-green   yellow-green

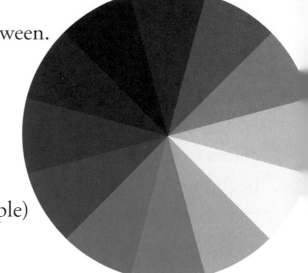

Warm and Cool Colors

Colors are grouped into "warm" and "cool" color families. **Warm colors** (WOHRM KUH lurz) are red, yellow, and orange and their related colors. Blue, green, and purple and colors like them are said to be cool colors (KOOL KUH lurz).

Warm Colors

To remember these warm colors, think of them as colors of the sun and of fire.

Cool Colors

To remember the cool color family, think of the colors that you would use to paint the icy waters of the Arctic regions.

Trace or make copies of these pictures on a copy machine. Use warm colors for one picture and cool colors for the other.

Value

Value (VAL yoo) refers to the darkness or lightness of a color. Contrasts between light and dark make certain objects in your painting stand out. They also add interesting things like shadows and highlights.

Notice how the look of your picture can change by changing the background color. The warm orange flower stands out more when painted on a contrasting, cool color.

Highlights and Shade

To figure out where highlights and shadows should be added, think of a beam of light or sunshine shining down from the top left side of your picture. Where would the light shine on the object, making it brighter? Where would the shadows fall?

Try This!

LIGHT

LIGHT

STEP 1

First lay down basic colors, adding shadows to the right side and under the ice cream scoop.

STEP 2

Now add both light and dark highlights to the ice cream and the cone. Study this picture and notice the white highlights added to the waffle cone.

Experiment with mixing colors on your palette, using your palette knife (a cotton swab or Popsicle stick will do) to apply dabs of paint. All the colors on the color wheel are **hues** (HYOOZ) of pure color. Notice that by adding white to colors you create a new **tint** (TINT) of that color. By adding black, you create a new **shade** (SHAYD) of that color. By adding gray you create a new tone of that color.

A value change gives you many choices of color.

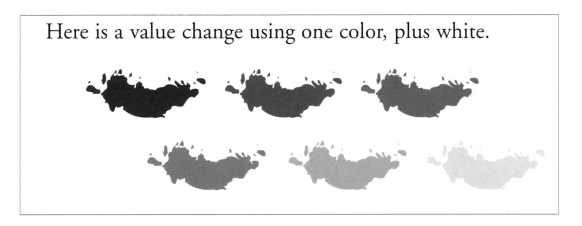

Here is a value change using one color, plus white.

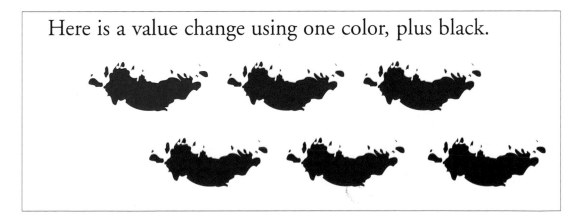

Here is a value change using one color, plus black.

Mixing Paint

With your palette knife, you can first mix the paints on your palette to get the colors you want before you apply them to your painting. Start with small amounts of paint; you can add more when you need it. Remember: it's very hard to return unused paint to the bottle! You can also mix paints directly on your paper, which is a little trickier and will take practice.

Cool Tips

Liquid tempera that has been stored can separate, so always shake the paint bottle *before* removing the lid.

16

Pointillism

You can apply paint in colors that complement one another (refer to the color wheel) in very small dots or dashes so close together that a viewer's eye "mixes" the paint as he stands back and looks at the picture. This painting technique is called **pointillism** (PWAHN tuh liz um) (painting with points of color), and was first used by an artist named Georges Seurat (suh RAH). Color television works in the same way, using dots of color that blend together on the screen.

Change your brush water frequently—dirty water will make the paint look dull and muddy in your painting.

Georges Seurat (1859-1891) mixed color using thousands of dots or "points" of paint placed closely together.

17

Try Pointillism Yourself!

STEP 1

Sketch out your picture. Then, start to fill in the objects with dots of color placed very, very close together. Use a tiny brush or a cotton swab. Remembering the colors of the color wheel, dab yellow and blue dots close together to create green, red and yellow dots to create orange, and red and blue dots to create purple.

STEP 2

As you add more and more points, the colors blend together to create new colors that make your painting look richer.

STEP 3

Red and blue dots placed close together give objects in your painting a shadowy effect.

What to Paint

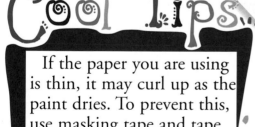

You may not be able to paint everywhere you go, but you can sketch in most places. Keeping a sketchbook is a great way to save ideas for painting. Your sketchbook can include simple doodles or drawings of interesting scenes or objects that you happen to see, or it may hold photos or even pictures cut out of magazines and newspapers.

Sketchbooks with hard covers and with unlined paper inside are best.

Cool Tips

If the paper you are using is thin, it may curl up as the paint dries. To prevent this, use masking tape and tape the corners of the paper to a piece of cardboard before applying paint. Do not remove until the painting is completely dry.

Artists' Secrets

Composition

Before you begin painting, stop and think about the picture's **composition** (kahm puh ZIH shun). Composition means the way the different parts of the picture will be composed, or its layout, and how they will relate to one another. You can use a viewfinder to zoom in on an object or scene you might want to paint.

A viewfinder is no more than a small frame that you can make out of cardboard. Use it to look through and determine what elements will go where in your picture. Where do you want the main object in your picture to be? Will your paper be horizontal or vertical?

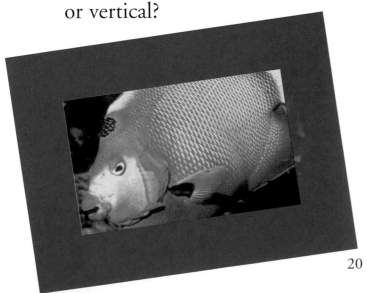

Good composition gives your painting "rhythm," which means the eyes of a person looking at your picture will move from one part of your picture to another in a pleasing, satisfying way. These are some "secrets" of good composition, and they will make your good painting even better:

Seeing Shapes

You learned about the basic shapes—square, circle, triangle, oval, and rectangle when you were very young. Look around you. Most every object you can think of is made up of a basic shape or can fit easily into a basic shape. Many objects are a combination of two, three, or more shapes, like a rectangular wagon and its four circular wheels.

Texture

When we speak of **texture** (TEKS chur), we think of something you can feel with your hand. An artist creates texture that you can feel with your eyes. By using different textures in your painting—looks that seem soft, hard, rough, smooth, fuzzy, irregular—you will make your art more interesting.

Sketch out the objects in your painting with a pencil before you start to paint. You can erase the lines later if you want.

Try Painting Smooth, Shiny Objects

STEP 1 Sketch an outline of the basic shapes in this picture. Outline the jar with white and blue, as indicated. Add bright color to gumballs, then paint in the table and background. Add white to soften the red background that shows through the jar.

STEP

2
Darker values of the colors you have used for the gumballs create shadows and highlights. A darker brown will give a wood grain effect to the table.

STEP

3
Continue to add light and dark highlights and shadows using different values of the same color. Add white dotted highlights to some of the gumballs.

Some artists, like the French painter Claude Monet (CLOD moh nay) (1840-1926), never used black in his paintings. To create shadows or other dark effects, he simply mixed dark colors like blue or green or purple.

Try Painting a Water Scene

STEP 1 Start with basic shapes and add flat color. You can sketch out the shapes first, if you like.

STEP 2 Like Monet, try to choose colors other than black for shading. The shadows under these waterlilies were created using a deep purple. Notice how adding a darker blue to some of the water toward the back of the picture in the second and third pictures creates a sense of depth.

STEP 3 Adding white highlights seem to give the water movement. Do you notice in the third picture that the same green used for the water lilies and the reeds is added to the water? Are the colors in this picture warm or cool?

Try Painting a Furry Animal

STEP 1

Lightly sketch the basic shapes in this picture. Fill the shapes with flat color.

STEP 2

Use short, fine strokes for the fur and the grass. You will need to use a thin brush. Use yellow and green for the grass, use orange and browns for the bears.

STEP 3

Now add darker colors over the shaded areas—a darker green for the grass, a darker brown for the bears' fur. Use different values of the same hue for the background grass. Finish your picture by adding cool colors to the shadows and warm colors to the highlights.

Lines and Patterns

Lines and patterns will give your picture interest, texture, and feeling. They will also keep the viewer's eyes moving from one point to another as they look at your painting. Lines can be thick, thin, spiral, radiating, jagged, curved, or whatever you like. You can experiment with lines in your painting to create different moods.

Vincent van Gogh (van GO) (1853-1890) used violent, swirling lines to express emotions in his paintings. This work, titled "Starry Night," was painted while Van Gogh was a patient in a mental hospital. He stayed up to paint three nights in a row in order to capture the colors of the night.

Try Making a Cool Art Supply Box!

STEP 1 Cover a medium or large shoe box with aluminum foil and tape the foil down inside the box to hold it in place.

STEP 2 Using powdered tempera, make a thick 1/2 cup of paint in one or more colors.

STEP 3 To each cup of thickened tempera, add 1 1/2 teaspoons of liquid dishwashing detergent and stir.

Paint the outside of your box with this mixture. The detergent helps the paint stick to the foil. Now you have a special box for your art supplies!

Cleanup

It only takes a few minutes to clean up after you've finished painting for the day and, as the artist, you are responsible for doing this.

1 Remove your still-wet painting from the easel (or table) and lay or hang it to dry, away from dirt, water, or curious pets.

2 Wipe up any paint spills in the painting area with a damp sponge. Before leaving the paint area, check the bottom of your shoes to make sure you have not stepped in paint!

3 Wash your brushes out well, pinch the pointed brushes to a point and flatten the flat brushes. Store all brushes with their handles down in an open container or place them flat in a drawer.

Do this...

...not this!

28

Make sure all the lids for the tempera bottles are on tight—liquid tempera can dry out easily.

4 Cover the tempera bottles tightly and store them together.

5 Put everything else away and wash your hands. You might use an old tackle box or something similar to keep your paint and paint tools together.

6 Don't forget to sign your painting!

Shiny Paint Recipe

For each color you want to use, mix together:
- 4 tablespoons of corn syrup
- 1 1/2 teaspoons of liquid dishwashing soap
- 1 1/2 teaspoons liquid tempera

Use a different cup to mix each color.

Paint your picture or design on cardboard. Your art will have a beautiful gloss when the paint dries!

Glossary

cool colors (KOOL KUH lurz) — "icy" colors such as greens, blues, violets

composition (kahm puh ZIH shun) — the arrangement of objects, shapes, color, and other elements in a painting

horizontal (hohr uh ZAHN tul) — a painting whose composition is more from side-to-side (like the horizon) than it is up-and-down

hue (HYOO) — another name for color

palette (PAL ut) — a flat surface or special tray used for mixing or thinning out paint; or the range of colors chosen by an artist for a particular work

palette knife (PAL ut NYF) — a tool used to mix or thin out colors on a palette

pointillism (PWAHN tuh liz um) — a style of painting that uses small dots and dashes of different colors placed closely together so they appear as yet another, more solid color

shade (SHAYD) — a dark value of a color; shading is on an object, as opposed to off the object like a shadow

tempera (TEM puh ruh) — a thick, inexpensive kind of paint that dries quickly and can be mixed with water

texture (TEKS chur) — the roughness or smoothness of a surface. Texture in a painting can actually be felt on the surface or simply seen in the painting.

tint (TINT) — any light value of a color; usually one color plus white added to it

value (VAL yoo) — refers to the lightness or darkness of a color

vertical (VUHR tuh kul) — a painting whose parts are composed more up-and-down than from side-to-side

warm colors (WOHRM KUH lurz) — colors of heat: reds, yellows, oranges

Index

Further Reading

- Brookes, Mona, *Drawing with Children*, G. P. Putnam's Sons,1996.
- Cummings, Pat, *Talking with Artists*, Simon & Schuster, 1992.
- Cummings, Pat, *Talking with Artists Vol. II*, Simon & Schuster, 1995.
- Davidson, Rosemary, *Take a Look: An Introduction to the Experience of Art*, Viking Press, 1994.
- Horton, James, *Composition*, Walter Foster Publishing, 1998.
- Kohl, Maryann, *Preschool Art*, Gryphon Press, 1994.
- King, Penny and Roundtree, Clare, *Portraits*, Crabtree Publishing, 1996.
- King, Penny and Roundtree, Clare, *Stories*, Crabtree Publishing, 1996.
- Martin, Judy, editorial consultant, *Painting and Drawing*, Millbrook, 1993.
- Martin, Mary, *Start Exploring Masterpieces*, Running Press. 1991.
- Thompson, Kimberly Boehler and Loftus, Diana Standing, *Art Connections*, GoodYear Books, 1995.

The
LOVINGS

The
LOVINGS
an intimate portrait

PHOTOGRAPHS BY   TEXT BY

GREY VILLET   **BARBARA VILLET**

FOREWORD BY STEPHEN CROWLEY

———

PRINCETON ARCHITECTURAL PRESS · NEW YORK

previous: **Richard and Mildred Loving**

Published by
Princeton Architectural Press
A McEvoy Group company
37 East Seventh Street
New York, New York 10003
202 Warren Street
Hudson, New York 12534
Visit our website at www.papress.com

Design: Ann Villet
Editor: Barbara Darko
Typesetting: Paul Wagner
Book producer: Valerie Tomaselli, MTM Publishing

Special thanks to: Janet Behning, Nicola Brower, Abby Bussel,
Erin Cain, Tom Cho, Benjamin English, Jenny Florence,
Jan Cigliano Hartman, Lia Hunt, Mia Johnson, Valerie Kamen,
Simone Kaplan-Senchak, Diane Levinson, Jennifer Lippert,
Kristy Maier, Sara McKay, Eliana Miller, Jaime Nelson Noven,
Esme Savage, Rob Shaeffer, Sara Stemen, and Joseph Weston
of Princeton Architectural Press —Kevin C. Lippert, publisher

Library of Congress Cataloging-in-Publication Data
Names: Villet, Grey, photographer. | Villet, Barbara, author.
Title: The Lovings : an intimate portrait / photographs by Grey Villet ; text
   by Barbara Villet.
Description: First edition. | New York : Princeton Architectural Press, 2017.
Identifiers: LCCN 2016039735 | ISBN 9781616895563 (hardback)
Subjects: LCSH: Families—Virginia—Pictorial works. | Loving, Richard
   Perry—Portraits. | Loving, Mildred Jeter—Portraits. | Loving, Richard
   Perry—Biography. | Loving, Mildred Jeter—Biography. | Interracial
   marriage—Virginia—Pictorial works. | Interracial marriage—Law and
   legislation—Virginia | BISAC: HISTORY / Social History. | PHOTOGRAPHY /
   Individual Photographers / Monographs. | PHOTOGRAPHY / Photoessays &
   Documentaries.
Classification: LCC TR681.F28 L68 2017 | DDC 779/.9306846 dc23
LC record available at https://lccn.loc.gov/2016039735

Foreword

Imagine, if you will, Grey Villet in his rural New York home at winter's end in 1966, carefully affixing the mailing address "Richard and Mildred Loving, Central Point, Virginia" onto a bulky 11" x 13" parcel of moments. Some fifty photographs, hand-printed in the *Life* magazine photo lab, filled the package—a gesture of friendship to the quiet and modest couple, who were challenging Virginia's ban on interracial marriage, from a quiet and modest man, who was one of the most influential practitioners of *Life*'s photographic essays.

In the spring of 1965, Mr. Villet had taken a *Life* assignment to photograph the Lovings, a married interracial couple then "embroiled in legal tangles after their arrest for miscegenation in the state of Virginia," as his wife and storytelling partner, Barbara Villet, later wrote. "Grey did not concern himself with those tangles; he chose, as he did in every essay we ever worked on together, to seek out the literal heart of the matter: a love story."

In 1967 the US Supreme Court upheld the right for couples of mixed race to marry. For the next seven years, the Lovings lived happily with their three children, bound by the love of each other and their extended family, until separated by the death of Richard, who was killed by a drunk driver in an automobile accident. Mildred, a quiet hero of the civil rights era, passed on May 2, 2008.

Over those intervening years, Grey's work on the Lovings had been shrouded by obscurity, and little had been written about him or it. Always unassuming, he had made no bid for attention during his long career, even forswearing entries in various photo competitions, believing, as he told Barbara, that in time "the work will tell" and find a lasting place in the annals of photojournalism. Tall, he was a man of few words whose subtle, comforting presence and preference for using only available light allowed him quietly to capture complex tableaus without disturbing his subjects, while carefully considering shutter speed and aperture. The results were such visceral scenes that it is difficult to remember they are only two-dimensional.

In this digital world, it's also easy to forget the kind of intensity of focus and experience it took to produce photographs like the ones Grey and his peers made, composing essays in the field without the benefit of the instant feedback available today. But Grey took the matter a step further in his search for veracity. "I hate to set up stuff," he told fellow *Life* photographer John Loengard in his book *What They Saw*. "I'd much rather let people act as they are, and reflect that. If I've got the patience, that'll give me a better picture than anything I can dream up."

I was nine years old, living in a small town in south Florida, when I read Grey Villet's 1961 "The Lash of Success" in *Life* magazine. *Life* was one of the very few extras my family could afford. Its pages were filled with images of President John F. Kennedy, the space program, and the rising stars of television. Yet it was the subject and style of "Lash"—about a businessman sacrificing his humanity in pursuit of success—that had the greatest impact upon me. It has always stayed with me, and I hold it partly responsible for my decision to pursue photography as a career. I've always believed that the proper way to honor artists' work is to respect their ideas while avoiding imitation, but it's difficult not to be influenced by Mr. Villet's oeuvre. I've done hundreds of picture stories since I started in photography in the late 1970s, and I have to admit that there's a bit of the Grey Villet DNA in every one of them.

—Stephen Crowley, photographer, *New York Times*, Washington Bureau, 2017

INTRODUCTION: A QUEST FOR JUSTICE

As the photographer Grey Villet listened to Mildred Loving explain how she and her husband, Richard, had become outlaws in the state of Virginia, neither could have predicted the lasting influence the story she was telling would have on America's future. It was April 1965 and Villet had come to the isolated farmhouse the Lovings had secretly rented in Virginia's King and Queen County, to do a story on their predicament for *Life* magazine. At the time, the Lovings, who were subject to as much as twenty-five years in prison if found living together in the state, were in the midst of challenging a Virginia law prohibiting their interracial marriage, one that reflected long-standing attitudes then common throughout the South supporting a separation of the races.

Villet was well acquainted with such attitudes. A South African by birth, he had seen apartheid instated there before emigrating to the United States to join *Life*, and his coverage of the violence attending the civil rights movement as it swept through Montgomery, Birmingham, Little Rock, and Memphis in the 1950s had made him well aware of the potential dangers of the Lovings' situation. Bombings, lynchings, cross burnings, and murders had answered early phases of the fight for racial equality, and although the Civil Rights Act of 1964 had outlawed many discriminatory practices at the federal level, it had not altered entrenched popular support for either extant state laws like that outlawing interracial marriage in Virginia or the common racial biases and resentments upholding them. But as Villet began to document their situation, its implicit dangers seemed something the Lovings had often managed to forget. As a result, the classic photographs collected here for the first time tell of a love story that is still influential in a changing America.

Mildred appeared resigned as she quietly described their situation on the first day that Villet and the *Life* reporter Bill Wise met with the couple. Richard remained silent as she spoke, but his face reflected a controlled fury toward their predicament as his wife outlined a story that stretched back seven years to their marriage in 1958. Under Virginia's anti-miscegenation law, the couple had been charged and jailed for the crime of being married, a felony that carried a penalty of one to five years in the state penitentiary. They had originally avoided jail time by pleading guilty to the crime and accepting banishment from Virginia under orders from the local circuit court's Judge Leon M. Bazile, not to return to the state together for twenty-five years. But after five years of hand-to-mouth exile in Washington, DC, they had decided to challenge their conviction legally, and in 1963 they returned secretly with their three children to the rented house in King and Queen County where Villet had found them.

Richard Loving and Mildred Jeter had grown up not far away, in Central Point in Virginia's Caroline County. Then little more than a hamlet in the rural northeastern corner of the state, it was home to a mixture of Rappahannocks, African Americans, and whites, who had a long history of quietly accommodating each other racially. The general attitude of the area on such matters was one of "live and let live," but the segregation laws of Virginia supporting racial separation were still enforced. Richard had gone to the all-white schools; Mildred, to those for mixed-race children. The laws that defined who went where were complex and antiquated.

In 1860 the Virginia General Assembly had codified what made individuals black, white, and Indian. Anyone with one-quarter African American ancestry was then defined as "negro," but by 1910 a "colored person" had been redefined as having just one-sixteenth or more of African American blood, while an "Indian" was anybody with one-quarter Native American ancestry. All of this had culminated in the Act to Preserve Racial Integrity, which the General Assembly passed in 1924, reaffirming prohibitions against interracial marriage but also radically limiting an individual's access to legal status as "white." "For the purpose of this act," the Assembly had declared, "the term 'white person' shall apply only to the person who has no trace whatsoever of any blood other than Caucasian." The only exception was for white elites who willingly still counted Pocahontas as an early ancestor.

Such arcane divisions were deeply embedded in Virginia's general society and severely limited the rights of nonwhites, not only in terms of schooling, but also in terms of access to restaurants, theaters, public transport, and even markets. But at twenty-five, Richard Loving, who was of Irish-English heritage, had fallen in love with then seventeen-year-old Mildred Jeter, a tall slim beauty of Native American and African American descent. After a yearlong courtship and the birth of their first son, Sidney, the two had gone to Washington, DC, to be legally married on June 2, 1958.

As Mildred recounted their story, she admitted that she had known of Virginia's rulings against interracial marriage, but in the belief that being legally joined in the District of Columbia would protect them, she had returned to Central Point with Richard to live in a small apartment in her mother's home. Legal authorities did not see it that way, however. Six weeks after the wedding, the county's attorney, Bernard Mahon, obtained a warrant for their arrest on a charge of violating Virginia's anti-miscegenation laws, and at two in the morning on July 13, Sheriff R. Garnett Brooks and two other officers broke into their apartment, awakening the sleeping couple. Challenged by Brooks, the Lovings indicated the wedding license they had hung on the wall beside their bed, and Mildred protested that she was Richard's wife. "Not here, you're not," the sheriff was said to have answered brusquely, before he arrested them both and transported them to the county jail in Bowling Green. The next day,

"I was scared to death." —Mildred Loving, recounting being in the county jail

Richard was freed on a $1,000 bond, but Mildred, whose family couldn't raise bail, languished alone in a cell for the next three days. Mildred would remember later how she had been "scared to death" after Richard's release, when Sheriff Brooks had escorted a male prisoner back into the jail from a work detail outside and told him, "I should let you go in here with her tonight." It was another two days before she was released to the custody of her father, Warren "Jake" Jeter.

Prohibited from living together, the couple remained apart officially until October, when a full indictment for their crime of being married was issued by the Caroline County Circuit Court. But not until January 1959, after the two meekly pleaded guilty, were those charges finalized. Judge Bazile then agreed to suspend their jail sentences on the condition that they leave Virginia and not return together for twenty-five years. By then their second son, Donald, had been born, and Mildred was expecting another child, their daughter Peggy, who arrived after they were exiled to Washington.

Often alone in a cousin's apartment with three young children while Richard was at work, Mildred grew increasingly unhappy. Though she made solo visits "home" to visit her own mother and Richard's over the next five years, the family's isolation in an unfamiliar city filled her with anxiety. By 1963, when then five-year-old Donald was grazed by a car in Washington's crowded streets, Mildred had become determined to get her three youngsters "home" to safe and familiar Caroline County, and she penned a plea for help to Attorney General Robert Kennedy. He responded by referring her to the local offices of the American Civil Liberties Union, which in turn enlisted Bernard S. Cohen, a youthful lawyer practicing in Alexandria, and Philip Hirschkop, an attorney only two years out of law school, to represent the Lovings in an appeal.

PART ONE: LOVE VS. THE LAW

As Mildred continued to explain to Villet and Wise during their initial meeting what had happened over the last several years, she unconsciously kept twisting her wedding band, as if to assure herself that it was still on her finger. Standing quietly apart and always intensely aware of fleeting signs of emotion, Villet caught the tensions of the moment on film. Richard, meanwhile, remained angrily silent, reluctant at first to make any comment on their situation. But over the following days, as Villet's unobtrusive manner allowed him almost to disappear as he began photographing them, the Lovings were lulled into normalcy. What began to emerge before his lenses was a portrait of them as a quintessentially ordinary couple extraordinarily in love with each other. She was a stay-at-home mom; he was a laborer who supported his family with his hands and his back. Their experiences, means, and ambitions were limited to what they had always known: the simplicity of a close family life in rural Central Point, where they had grown up as part of a racially inclusive working class. Far from being civil rights activists, as they would often later be described, they were motivated entirely by personal reasons. All they wished for was the freedom to live together as husband and wife, at home, near their family and friends.

In the spring of 1965, however, the thought that wanting such a simple thing might become an issue for the highest court in the land lay beyond the Lovings' considerations. Richard continued to hope that a new approach to Judge Bazile might resolve their difficulties, but in general he devoted himself to Mildred, his children, and his other great love, cars. Mildred found solace in the care of her young children and Richard's abiding affection, but she was ever-conscious of the perils they faced.

The Lovings had rented the hideaway house in King and Queen County under a false name, but it remained dangerous for them to be seen in public together elsewhere. Moreover, since Mildred did not have a car, she was limited to staying there with the three children most of the time. Richard, meanwhile, left the family alone daily when he went to work, and his departure was always difficult for his wife. She would worry if an unknown car pulled into their yard or if Richard was late coming home, and would occasionally give in to the tears she tried to hide. During their early stay at the house, she had been so fearful of their being found that she often stayed up until four in the morning so she could run away if a strange car appeared.

In time, her aging father, Jake Jeter, came to live with them, and both of their mothers made visits, but the uncertainty of their situation persisted. As Easter approached that April, a return to family homes in Central Point had to be carefully orchestrated for them to arrive separately, although they occasionally made daring stops together at a small general store nearby, where the proprietor was a friend. Otherwise, if they needed to visit a supermarket or purchase other supplies, it required a long trip to Tappahannock, where they were strangers. But after two years in hiding, sustained by the gentle domesticity they shared as a family and weekend escapes to the Sumerduck Dragway, where Richard raced a dragster he and his closest friends, Ray Green and Percy Fortune, had rebuilt, the couple had come to live within the constraints and cope with the dangers of their predicament. When questioned about what he would do if discovered defying Bazile's orders, Richard was adamant. "I won't divorce her," he replied firmly. "We'll move away again if we have to."

"I won't divorce her. We'll move away again if we have to." —Richard Loving

17

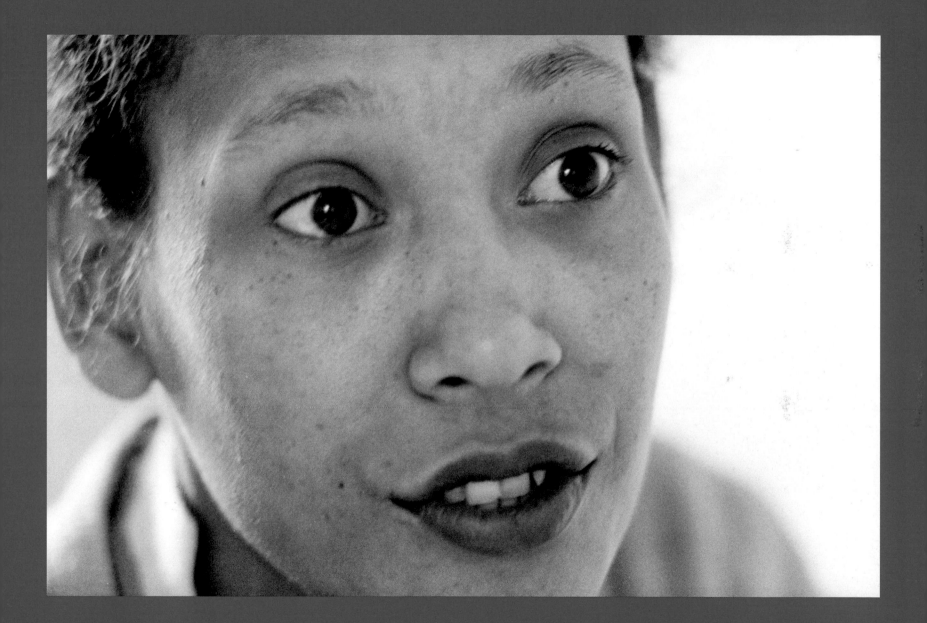

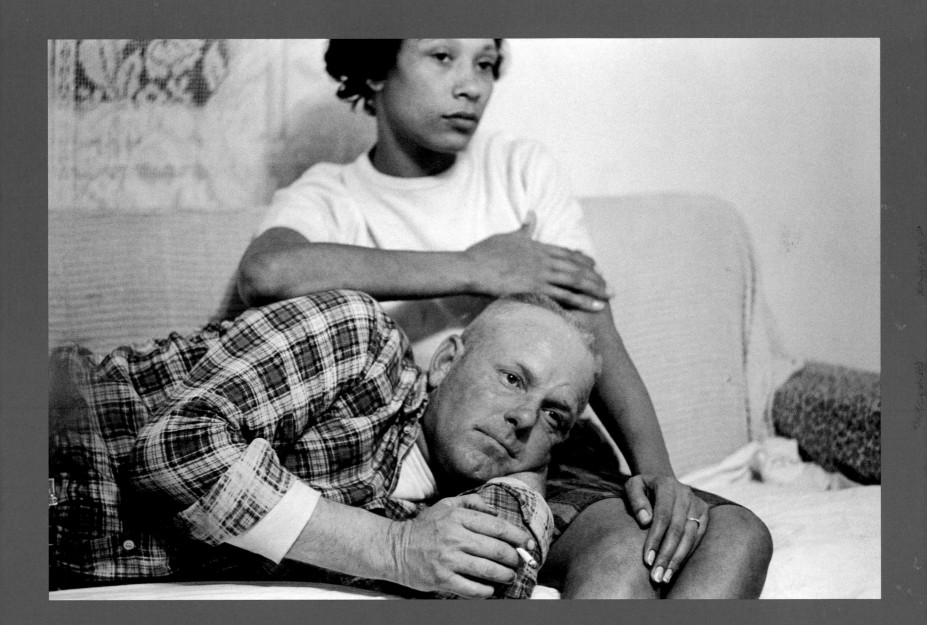

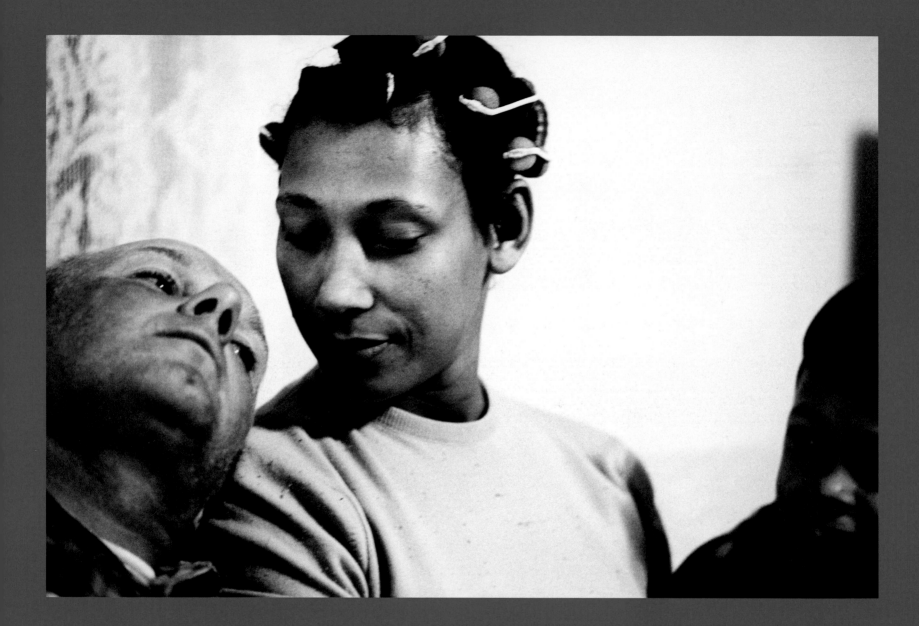

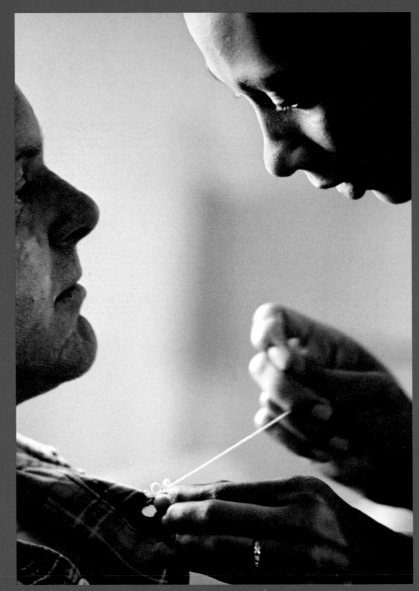

Peggy sleeps in her mother's arms.

Richard and coworkers take a lunch break.

Far left: Richard at work; left and above: Richard and Ray Green work on a dragster.

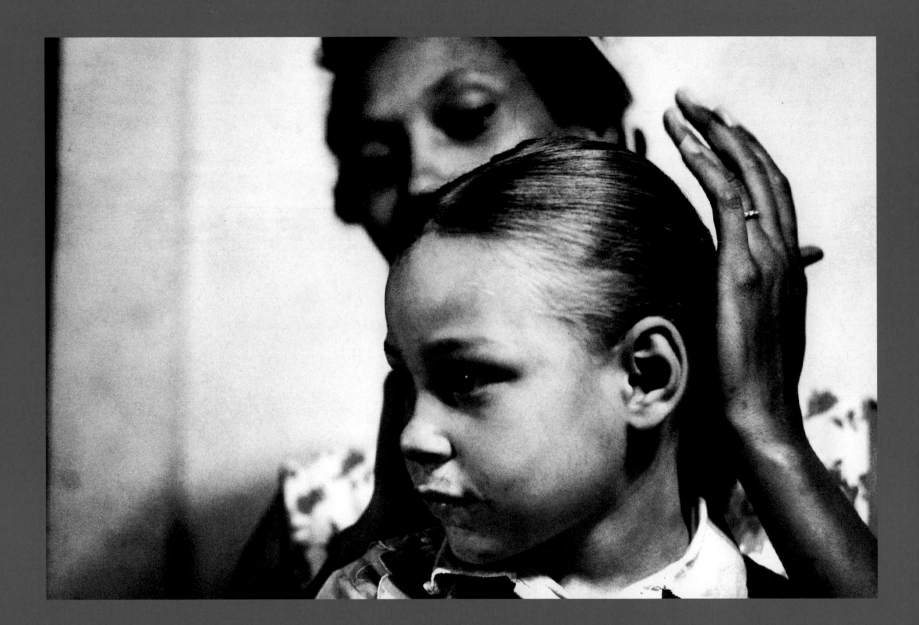

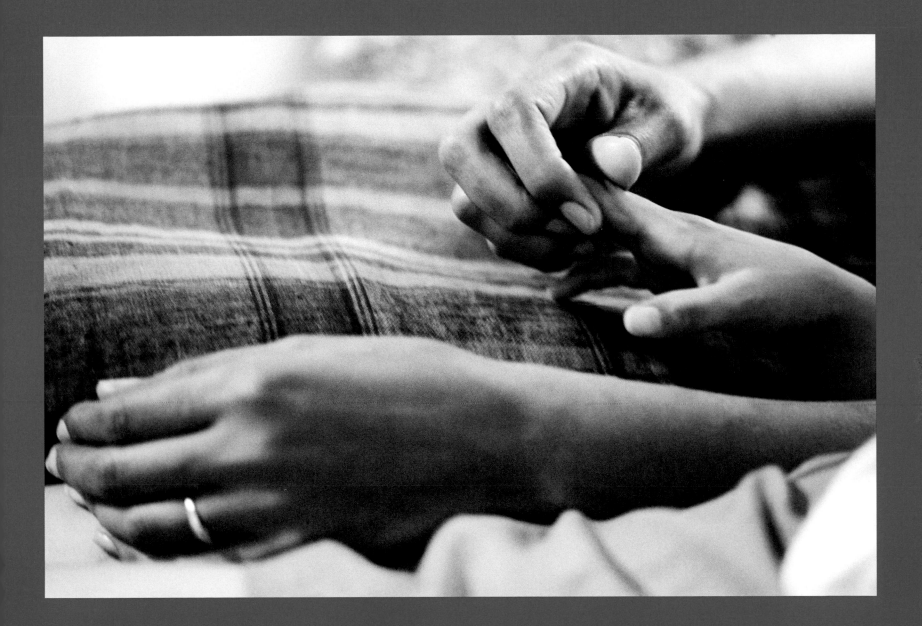

Donald, Peggy, and Sidney watch a favorite show while waiting for Richard to come home.

Mildred and Richard drop in to chat with friends at Joe Tignor's general store in Passing, Virginia.

The Lovings shop in Tappahannock, Virginia, outside the Caroline County line.

PART TWO: THE LAW

By 1965, the Lovings and their lawyers were still struggling with Virginia's courts. As the case moved slowly forward, each request for a meeting in Cohen and Hirschkop's Alexandria offices created renewed anxiety for the Lovings, which sometimes spilled over into Richard quarreling with Mildred. Following Cohen's 1963 request to Judge Bazile's court that the Lovings' original conviction be set aside, Bazile had delayed his response until 1965. But by dodging the constitutional issues of the case, the court had opened the way for the Lovings' lawyers to take their case to Virginia's Supreme Court of Appeals. Before that, however, the case reached a pivotal point: in January 1965, Judge Bazile, backed by the Commonwealth's attorney for Caroline County, J. Peyton Farmer, finally answered Cohen's earlier motion.

Refusing to vacate his initial conviction of the Lovings, he wrote a racially charged response: "Almighty God created the races white, black, yellow, malay and red, and he placed them on separate continents. And but for the interference with his arrangement there would be no cause for such marriages. The fact that he separated the races shows that he did not intend for the races to mix." Both appealable and inflammatory, this decision introduced religious and moral elements into the case that would eventually benefit the Lovings' lawyers as the appeals process began in Virginia's Supreme Court of Appeals.

Over these many months, visits to Cohen and Hirschkop for depositions continued to remind the couple of the seriousness of their situation, especially after a number of worrisome incidents. Both lawyers had begun receiving threatening phone calls; their cars were vandalized; the Ku Klux Klan's newspaper published disparaging references to "two Jew lawyers"; other members of the Virginia bar were overtly cold to them. But the most troubling event came when Klansmen rallied to burn a cross near Mildred's mother's home in Central Point as the case moved toward a hearing by Virginia's Supreme Court of Appeals.

The critical judgment the court delivered on March 7, 1966, upheld as legitimate Virginia's right "to preserve the racial integrity of its citizens" and to prevent "the corruption of blood" that could result in "a mongrel breed of citizens" and "the obliteration of racial pride." The ruling not only refuted the personal issues of freedom and fairness that had prompted the Lovings original challenge to the law, it was also so contrary to the proscription against invidious racial discrimination contained in the due process clause of the Fourteenth Amendment that it cleared the way for their lawyers to take their appeal to the US Supreme Court.

"Tell the court I love my wife, and it is just unfair that I can't live with her in Virginia." —Richard Loving, to attorney Bernard S. Cohen

On April 10, 1967, almost two years to the day after Villet had begun work on a photo-essay that still stands as silent testimony to the love story at the heart of the Lovings' case, the US Supreme Court began hearing the case. When asked if he wished to attend, Richard admitted he neither understood nor cared about the constitutional implications of the case, and both Richard and Mildred declined to be present at the opening arguments. Representing Virginia, the assistant attorney general, Robert McIlwaine, insisted that even if Virginia's laws seemed contrary to the Fourteenth Amendment, they were legitimate because they protected the state from the "sociological, psychological evils which attend interracial marriages." Citing research that suggested "that intermarried families are subjected to much greater pressures and problems than those of the intramarried," he argued further that they should be prohibited on the grounds that they were damaging to children.

Contesting such arguments, Hirschkop asserted that by denying the Lovings and their children their civil rights solely because of race, the state was not only in violation of the Constitution, but that its Act to Preserve Racial Integrity was nothing more than an extension of slavery laws, and "not concerned with the racial integrity of the Negro race, only with the white race." However, the most dramatic moment in the hearings occurred when Cohen spoke. "No matter how we articulate this," he told the justices, "no matter which theory of the due process clause or which emphasis we attach to, no one can articulate it better than Richard Loving when he said to me, 'Mr. Cohen, tell the court I love my wife and it is just unfair that I can't live with her in Virginia.'"

On June 12, 1967, the Supreme Court ruled unanimously in favor of the Lovings, striking down Virginia's racial purity laws on marriage, and ultimately those of sixteen other states, for violating the due process clause of the Fourteenth Amendment. Chief Justice Earl Warren wrote the landmark opinion, in which he not only quoted the inflammatory statements that Judge Bazile had made when he refused to vacate his initial conviction of the Lovings, but also went on to describe marriage as "one of the 'basic civil rights of man,' fundamental to our very existence and survival. To deny this fundamental freedom on so unsupportable a basis as the racial classifications embodied in these statutes, classifications so directly subversive of the principle of equality at the heart of the Fourteenth Amendment, is surely to deprive all the State's citizens of liberty without due process of law." It was a finding that would resonate far into the future and bear on issues of marriage and gender equality that remain current to this day. But in 1967, what the court's decision did for the Lovings was simple: it set them free at last to go home to a house Richard had built for Mildred and his family close to their parents and friends.

Richard's mother, Lola Loving (left), stands with Peggy and Mildred's sister Garnet in the background, behind Mildred and Richard.

Virginia was one of only sixteen states that prohibited interracial marriage in 1967. Penalties for miscegenation arose as a result of slavery and, since colonial times, had been routine in Virginia.

The Lovings meet attorney Bernard S. Cohen at his office in Alexandria, Virginia.

Far left: J. Peyton Farmer, Commonwealth attorney for Caroline County; left: Caroline County judge Leon M. Bazile; above: Judge Bazile at home.

In 1965, two years into the appeal of Judge Bazile's first ruling, the case would be heard by Virginia's Supreme Court of Appeals. Its ruling the following year opened the way to a hearing at the Supreme Court of the United States.

Attorneys Bernard S. Cohen and Philip Hirschkop discuss the case with the Lovings.

PART THREE: AN ESCAPE TO FREEDOM

When Richard asked Cohen to tell the court that he found it "just unfair" that Virginia's laws prohibited his marriage to Mildred, he had touched upon values of freedom and fairness that were key to his character. Richard was a man of quietly independent spirit; it was not surprising, therefore, that an important escape from the constraints of the Lovings' legal entanglements for him had been getting away from it all at the Sumerduck Dragway. The traditions of racial diversity and fairness that prevailed at drag strips like Sumerduck were familiar to Villet, who realized that attending races there would represent a needed escape to freedom for both Lovings. At Sumerduck, where speed was freedom for Richard and freedom was happiness for both, the Lovings were entirely themselves, open in their public displays of affection and emotionally at home as part of a mixed group of close friends.

Chief among this group was Ray Green, Richard's best friend. Ray, Richard, and Percy Fortune had partnered to rebuild a dragster, and the three had brought it to race at Sumerduck, where a following of friends and family from Central Point was on hand to celebrate. It was while they were waiting for results of a qualifying race that one of the track judges made a call that Richard thought unfair. Reacting with a rare display of temper that suggested the kind of stubborn will which also informed his larger fight with the state, he suddenly drove his car out onto the track, stopping all action, until the judge's decision was reversed. It was a small victory, but an emotionally significant one for Richard, because it corrected what he believed was another unjust judgment. The Loving team were regulars at Sumerduck, and that day they added another trophy to a collection that would earn them national recognition. According to a September 1967 article in *Ebony* titled "The Couple That Rocked the Courts," they were "one of the country's most successful integrated drag racing partnerships," spending $4,000 on their specially equipped dragster, and earning $2,700 and thirty-eight trophies in 1966 alone.

Percy Fortune (second from left), Richard, Ray Green (right, back to camera), and friends survey a dragster engine.

Ray Green (left), Percy Fortune (center), and Richard ready their car to race.

PART FOUR: LOVE

Past and future were blended in Grey Villet's classic photo-essay on the Lovings. What they were for each other, their children, and their families in 1965, they would continue to be in the years that remained to them after the 1967 Supreme Court decision. The only objective of their decision to challenge Virginia's anti-miscegenation laws had been to be recognized as legally married and allowed to go home freely.

By the time of Villet's visit, they had already achieved part of that goal by secretly moving back to Virginia in defiance of its laws, in order to return their children to the kind of country life and freedom that had fostered their own independent spirits. But otherwise, the Lovings had contested none of the state's other problematic dictates, including those that still required them to send their eldest son, Sidney, to a school for mixed-race children, where Peggy and Donald were soon to follow. Instead, what they still hoped for in 1965 was simply to return to live as a married couple near their families and friends in the small community in which they had grown up.

Richard's mother's home in Central Point was already a safe retreat for them. His mother, Lola Loving, a close and caring ally for her son, was also more than Mildred's mother-in-law. She had been midwife to the birth of all three of her grandchildren and had a special relationship with each of them. Mildred's own mother, Musiel, along with her sister Garnet and her other siblings lived across the street from Lola, and family gatherings for haircuts at the Jeter home often ended with inclusive, impromptu parties. Beyond their families, the couple had also managed a secret social life, cruising the country roads around Central Point with friends like Ray Green and other members of their close circle.

So it was that, in spite of the far-reaching legal impact of the 1967 Supreme Court decision in their case, little change came to the Lovings' personal lives. Once they were declared legally married, they had simply gone home with their children to live in a modest concrete block house that Richard had built for Mildred just up the road from her mother in Milford, close to Central Point. There the family had retreated into a well-guarded domesticity, until their quiet life together was abruptly cut short in 1975, when Richard was killed in an automobile accident that also took one of Mildred's eyes.

Left a widow, Mildred became increasingly reclusive and unassuming, insisting in rare interviews that what she and Richard had done, they had done "only for themselves" and not as civil rights activists. Nevertheless, in 2007, when a gay rights group advocating for marriage equality requested her help, Mildred allowed a rare public statement in her name. "I believe all Americans, no matter their race, no matter their sex, no matter their sexual orientation, should have that same freedom to marry.… I am still not a political person," she insisted, "but I am proud that Richard's and my name is on a court case that can help reinforce the love, the commitment, the fairness, and the family that so many people, black or white, young or old, gay or straight seek in life. I support the freedom to marry for all. That's what Loving, and loving, are all about."

"I support the freedom to marry for all. That's what Loving, and loving, are all about."
—Mildred Loving

Mildred died at home on May 2, 2008. Her daughter, Peggy, the last of her children still living, later recalled that the few times her mother spoke about the past in her final years was when she took comfort from the set of photographs Grey Villet had sent as a personal gift to the Lovings. Those same images of a loving past are reproduced here from the original negatives as part of the complete photo-essay by Villet, published for the first time in this volume.

Peggy and Donald visit a classroom during a fair at the mixed-race school they will be required to attend.

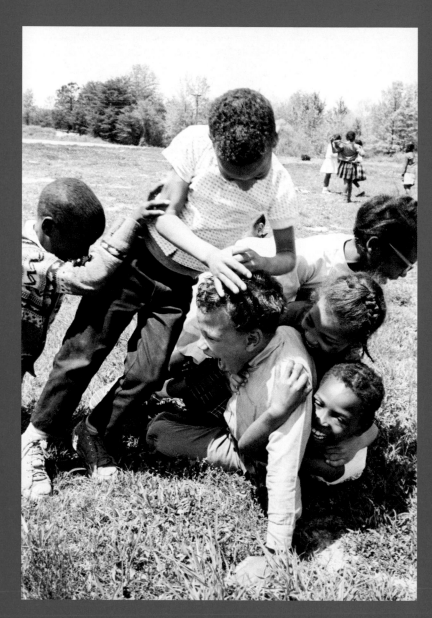

Above: At the fair, Peggy befriends a fellow student.
Right: Her brothers and friends wrestle.

Richard, Mildred, Donald, and Peggy visit the home of Richard's mother, Lola Loving (center).

Peggy receives a haircut at the home of Mildred's mother, Musiel Jeter, across the street from Lola Loving's house.

Fellow car-lover and neighbor John Ellis drops in for a visit.

STATEMENT BY MILDRED LOVING, 2007

Statement by Mildred Loving, June 12, 2007

Excerpted from "Loving for All," commemorating the fortieth anniversary of the *Loving v. Virginia* decision and in support of the Massachusetts ruling in favor of marriage equality for same-sex couples:

My generation was bitterly divided over something that should have been so clear and right. The majority believed...what the judge said, that it was God's plan to keep people apart, and that government should discriminate against people in love. But I have lived long enough now to see big changes. The older generation's fears and prejudices have given way, and today's young people realize that if someone loves someone they have a right to marry.

Surrounded as I am now by wonderful children and grandchildren, not a day goes by that I don't think of Richard and our love, our right to marry, and how much it meant to me to have that freedom to marry the person precious to me, even if others thought he was the "wrong kind of person" for me to marry. I believe all Americans, no matter their race, no matter their sex, no matter their sexual orientation, should have that same freedom to marry. Government has no business imposing some people's religious beliefs over others. Especially if it denies people's civil rights.

I am still not a political person, but I am proud that Richard's and my name is on a court case that can help reinforce the love, the commitment, the fairness, and the family that so many people, black or white, young or old, gay or straight seek in life. I support the freedom to marry for all. That's what Loving, and loving, are all about.

Dedication

This book is dedicated to the family—all families everywhere, made up of similar and different parents, of all colors, races, and genders. In particular, this book is dedicated to the family of Mildred and Richard Loving, who made it possible for so many of today's families to live without fear. This book is also dedicated to the memory of Grey Villet and to his family. Without the work of Grey Villet, the Lovings' story would not be so alive as it is today.